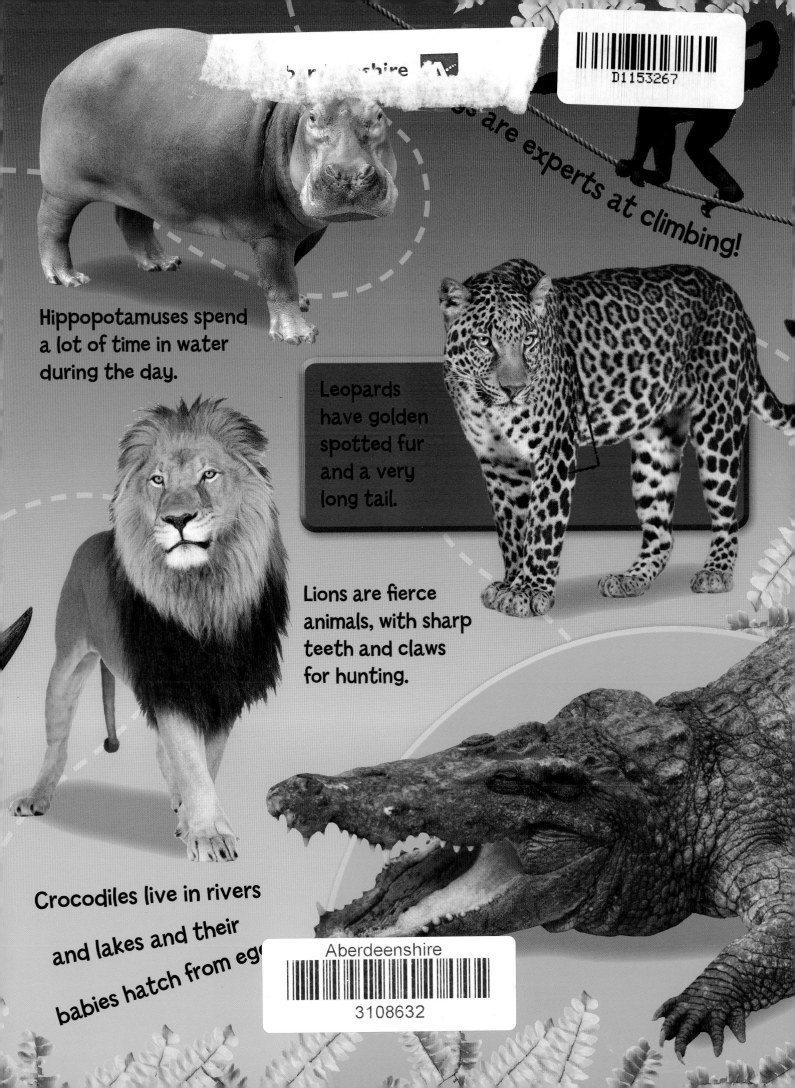

...are experts at climbing!

Hippopotamuses spend a lot of time in water during the day.

Leopards have golden spotted fur and a very long tail.

Lions are fierce animals, with sharp teeth and claws for hunting.

Crocodiles live in rivers and lakes and their babies hatch from eggs.

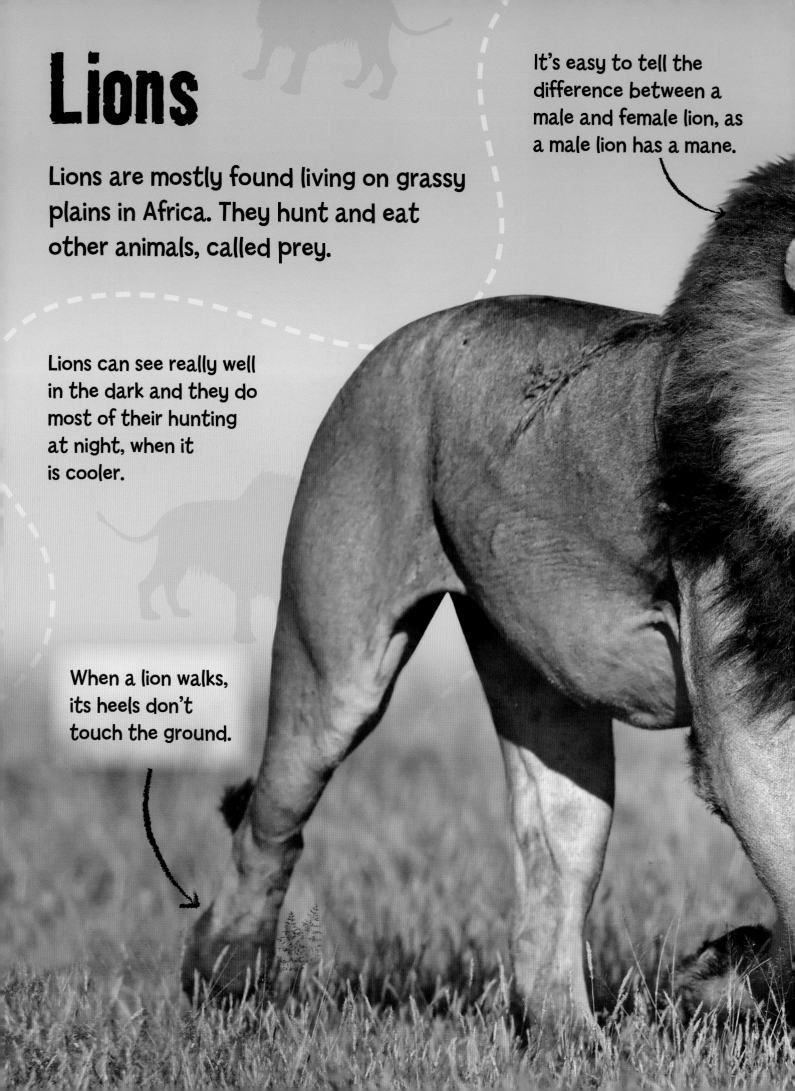

Lions

Lions are mostly found living on grassy plains in Africa. They hunt and eat other animals, called prey.

It's easy to tell the difference between a male and female lion, as a male lion has a mane.

Lions can see really well in the dark and they do most of their hunting at night, when it is cooler.

When a lion walks, its heels don't touch the ground.

Lionesses are more agile than the male lions. They hunt in groups on the plains.

Lions live in large family groups, called prides.

A lion's roar can be heard 5 miles away!

Elephants

A group of elephants is called a herd.

Elephants are the largest of all living land mammals. The African elephant is not only taller and heavier than the Asian elephant, it also has bigger ears and more wrinkled skin.

Elephants use their long trunks to reach leaves and branches high up in the trees.

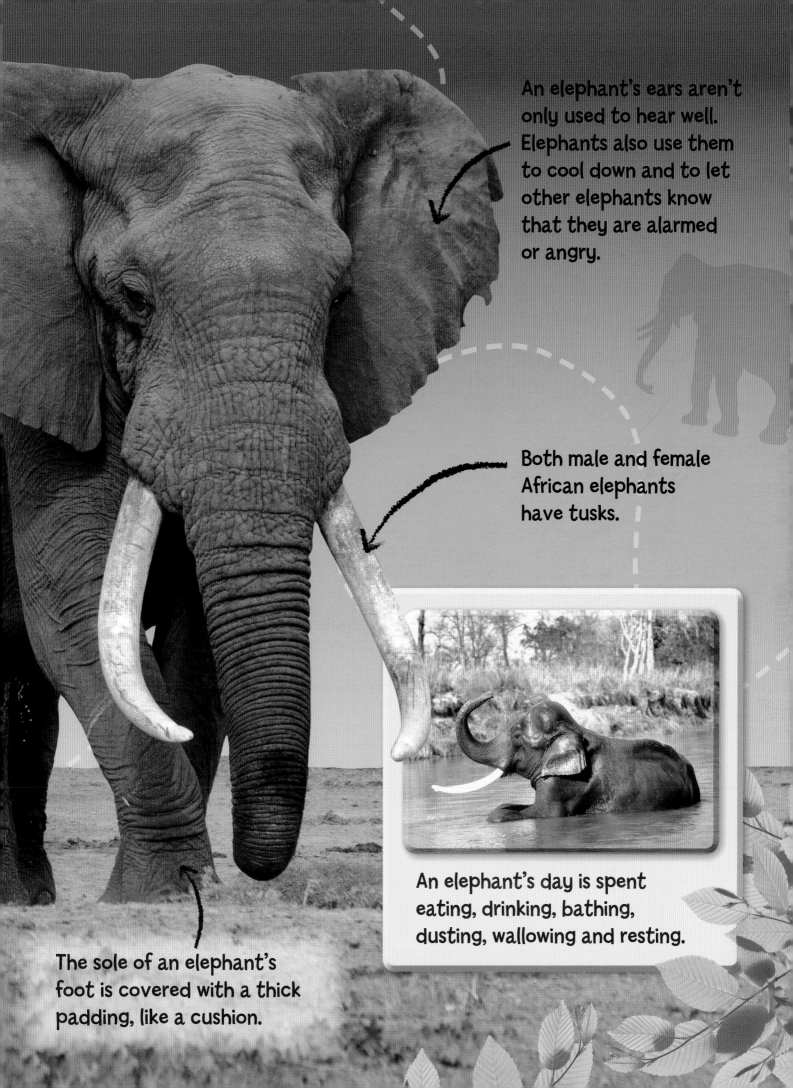

An elephant's ears aren't only used to hear well. Elephants also use them to cool down and to let other elephants know that they are alarmed or angry.

Both male and female African elephants have tusks.

An elephant's day is spent eating, drinking, bathing, dusting, wallowing and resting.

The sole of an elephant's foot is covered with a thick padding, like a cushion.

Under the sea

Starfish usually have five arms and live at the bottom of the sea.

Sharks are large fish with sharp teeth and an excellent sense of smell.

Octopuses have eight legs, called tentacles.

Some turtles can live for over 100 years!

Seals are excellent swimmers and spend most of their time in water.

Killer whales have teeth that can be as long as 10cm!

snap!

A seahorse uses its long tail to hold on to underwater plants.

Lobsters live on the ocean floor and can catch fish with their claws.

Most crabs can only walk sideways!

Whales

Whales are huge mammals that live in the sea. There are many different species including the blue whale, humpback whale, and sperm whale.

Humpback whales are pregnant for 11–12 months and give birth to just one baby, called a calf.

Scientists now believe that some whales can live as long as 200 years!

All whales use their flippers for balance and steering.

A whale breathes air through a blowhole on its head when it gets to the surface.

Some whales have teeth and some don't. Whales that don't have teeth are called baleen whales.

A group of whales is called a pod.

Geese are large birds that live in groups called a gaggle.

A pig has a flat nose, a thick body and short legs.

Horses can sleep both lying down and standing up.

Not all sheep are kept on farms. In some countries sheep live on hills and mountains.

Donkeys can live for over 40 years.

A female chicken, called a hen, lays eggs and then sits on them to keep them warm.

Hee-haw!

Cows

Cows live in fields and spend most of their day grazing on grass. Farmers keep cows for their milk or for their meat.

Black and white cow markings are unique - no two cows have exactly the same pattern.

A cow uses its long tail to keep flies away.

Milk can be made into other food such as yoghurt, cheese and butter.

While humans have five toes on each foot, cows only have two.

A baby cow is called a calf. A cow has her first calf when she is about two years old.

MOOO!

Most of the milk we drink comes from cows.

Sheep

Sheep are mainly kept for their wool and meat, although some farmers keep sheep for their milk.

Lambs are usually born in the springtime.

Each year, as the weather gets warmer, a sheep's fleece is shorn off and made into wool yarn.

The wool covering a sheep's body is called a fleece.

Sheep live in big groups called flocks or herds.

A sheep's toenails are called hooves.

Tortoises are plant eaters and have no teeth.

Just like human finger nails a rabbit's teeth never stop growing.

This dwarf hamster fills its cheeks with food to take back to its nest.

Fish have gills that they use to breathe.

A dog's sense of smell is much better than a human's.

Cats are good at seeing in the dark and can hear very well, too.

Guinea pigs' ears are very sensitive to strange and sudden noise.

A mouse's tail is usually as long as its body.

Cats

Cats are one of the most popular pets in the world. They are usually short-haired or long-haired and can live until they are between 12 and 15 years old.

A cat usually has about 12 whiskers on each side of its face.

Baby cats, called kittens, are usually born in litters of between two and six.

To help them hunt in the dark, cats have powerful night vision and excellent hearing.

Cats have flexible bodies and sharp teeth and claws.

Cats use their tails to help them balance.

Cats spend a large amount of time licking their coats to keep them clean.

Cats sleep a lot - as much as 20 hours a day!

Dogs

Dogs are often called 'man's best friend' because dogs help humans in many different ways. Some are kept as working animals, others as family pets.

Because their ears are more sensitive than ours, dogs can hear sounds that humans can't.

Dogs have been kept by humans for over 10,000 years.

Dogs wag their tails when they are happy or excited.